FURTHER ADVENTURES WITH YOU

C.D. Wright

Carnegie-Mellon University Press
Pittsburgh 1986

Acknowledgments

Grateful acknowledgment is made to the following publications in which some of these poems first appeared: *Black Warrior Review, Brown Journal of the Arts, Field, Five Fingers Review, Imagine: edicion feminista, Ironwood, racoon, Three Rivers Poetry Journal;* "Wages of Love," "Treatment," "Elements of Night," and "The Wooden Age" first appeared in *TriQuarterly,* a publication of Northwestern University. "Carla", "Slag", and "hills" first appeared in Poetry East. *"This Couple"* is reprinted by permission of *The New Yorker,* © 1985 The New Yorker Magazine, Inc.

The publication of this book is supported by grants from the National Endowment for the Arts in Washington, D.C., a Federal agency, and by the Pennsylvania Council on the Arts.

Carnegie-Mellon University Press books are distributed by Harper and Row.

Contents

for my parents and for my brother Warren

Lives are delicate things. Anything could happen . . . . People fall.

Meredith Steinbach

hills

People were going around with chickenfeet.
People were going around with bibles. "History of John Stoss," Frank Stanford

There was plenty of loud talk at the table, late corn, continuous palaver in other parts of the house; a handsome brother with principles and the future on his mind, who came in good time to counsel the mentally unbalanced. None of the Wrights so far as that goes are inordinately stable. Or else, neurotically so. We are a smart bunch. Verbal down to the altogether illiterate. 1949, the year stoically captioned by one poet as "A whore blowing smoke in the dark," I was born. On Epiphany, a podalic version. "You tore me up," my mother swore, "No more," and her womb blew back into the trees. My first words—I've been told—were obscene. My highchair was handed-down and painted over white. I remember the hard heels of my white shoes chipping at the paint of the rung. Brought up in a large unaestheticized house littered with *Congressional Records* and stenotype paper by a Chancery Judge and The Court's hazel-eyed Reporter who took down his every word, which was law. Throughout my childhood I was knife-sharp and aquatic in sunlight. I read.

There was an impotent public education, never enough music in the home, not enough bathrooms. Books in heaps under beds, on the lid of stools, on the formica counter and the dining table with the cat who had lost its tail hair. After "lights out" I tunneled into the closet onto a wad of abused fluffy toys and plaid schooldresses with *The Razor's Edge, Jo's Boys, The Olde Curiosity Shoppe, Pride & Prejudice,* a Nancy Drew mystery, *The Fountainhead* (I wasn't particular), and pages and pages to go...

Lived in Ozarks until I was seventeen. Typically young, American and miserable. Then I moved: Vicksburg, Springfield, Memphis, New York, Atlanta—going to colleges and working until 1972 when I returned to attend graduate school at the University of Arkansas, Fayetteville where I stayed until 1979. Too long. Now those tangles have been combed out, and I still have most of my hair, I can say, I am largely Ms. Vittitow-educated but cannot stop to explain. That is, she was critical, and I can't adequately cipher the layers of her space, time, causality, much less the uncanny way whereby she took literature in whole and gave it back lustrous and living.

The geographic sovereignty of my state of origin goes unchallenged by me. For its natural resources, no other single land mass is more suited to being a country than Arkansas. And were such a thing to come to pass, no other country would more resemble the dread South Africa. For that mattter, I haven't met with much of well-heeled America exempt from such a comparison. In the case of Arkansas I do not miss the persistence of tar-paper siding, segregation, right-to-work laws, dried-apple dolls, religious disturbances, or the screened and lagging informational flow. Not the dominion of football. Those HOGS were lost on me. At no point was I interested in the care and feeding of grown chickens. But among the many elements I do miss, which if not in bounty, survive, no, thrive, in pockets; so, it isn't mere nostalgia to name them: four full and even seasons, hardwood and green waterways, mockingbirds, barges, berry jellies, the Missouri Pacific line, one-lane bridges, variety gardens. I pine for the shade-tree ingenuity and speech of its citizens, Sunday's *Gazette,* along with a diurnal faith in the earth's near permanence which residence in the interior permits.

The particulars of hill society have shaped my work more than any certain somebody. Re-reading the *Writer's Project Guide to the State*, published first in 1941, and extrapolating from descriptions of individual hill women, I have no trouble spotting myself: bony but strong as a weed, an abiding refusal to smile or sing; a relentless if not brutal honesty; streaks of the mean, the grotesque in humor. Thomas Hardy's descriptions of the peasant yeomanry of England, quoted in the same guide, are likewise faithful to my relations: "blond, grey-eyed, slim, with straight mouths, determined chins, independent and hidebound, adaptable to circumstances, free of outside influences, not complacent, and don't fight well unless cornered. Then to the death." In my family until my parents' generation, all were dirt farmers on the father's side, railroad workers on the mother's. Both sides have taken root in the most stubborn sense of the word in similar topography for a couple hundred years: Alleghenies, Blue Ridge, Smokies, Ozarks; with a scant sampling forging as far West as the Oklahoma Badlands.

Creation is forward-looking even when the setting is bygone, and I have known many get-cracking artists from the Ozarks: visual, plastic, musical, literary and I continue to know and honor their work as it changes and grows. Some have stayed on, more have moved off. I resent the city which goes uninformed by the country, or which minds the woods only long enough to pluck out a naif to pronounce visionary, to patronize for a flash and just as promptly forget. I hate to see someone whose imagination is pure, *taken* by someone whose careerist intentions are obscene. Similarly I feel discouraged when the country is too incestuous and defensive to recognize the living intelligence of the city. I aim to carry the smoked ham of my voice to Beulahland. I do not intend to write as though I had not gotten wind of "this here" or "that there" semiotic theory, regardless of which if any one theory, prevails.

The last book I completed, *Translations Of The Gospel Back Into Tongues,* is a lamentation for the late Frank Stanford, poet from Arkansas, and a tribute to the great American experience of jazz. It is told in that odd way I have. But my life, ergo my life's work is not the same now as it was then. A year after Stanford's death I moved, in near ruins, to San Francisco. Literarily, the cumulative effect of what I've been laid open to here has been at the outset paralyzing. But I am beginning to walk upright again; to see what they have out here I can take back for my fire. I will not say this hasn't been reciprocal, that Californians have not been interested in a country perspective. But once, after a reading, I overheard a man say to another man, "She's a real one, a real hillbilly." I thought he was a patronizing fart, but I am, irrevocably, a purebred hill person. I do not see the literary life as being either scalded from or hidebound by that fact.

When I began to write seriously I wrote strictly dialect with aberrant spelling, subject-verb disagreements...I wrote blue tick hounds accompanied by untunable git-tars and ocarinas (a simple wind instrument known in the vernacular as the sweet potato). Until recently my writing has continued to reflect the pitch of that speech. Now that I can recognize it from the outside, I can reproduce it at will, but am no longer committed to pursuing a course whereby my language is rife with *idiom Ozarkia.* I mean I can only yammer and yarn my way through so many hundreds of lines, living as I do between the Wisconsin Street Housing Project and the San Jose Freeway, in a flat that oversees the shipyards of Bethlehem Steel. It is a warboat they are assembling at the water's edge, a far cry from midwifery in Leslie or Evening Shade (a community alternately called Hookrum). While I prefer cornbread crumbled in buttermilk to sushi I do not write from my lost life alone, any more than I dictate every term by which I do write.

My poems are about desire, conflict, the dearth of justice for all. About persons of small means. They are succinct but otherwise orthodox novels in which the necessary characters are brought out, made intimate (that is, they reveal themselves), engage in dramatic action and leave the scene forever with or without a resolution in hand or sight. Each on the space of a page or less. Obversely, my prose is private, meditative; without a cast, discernible intention, goal or dramatic fulcrum. My prose is about language if it is about any one thing. It is possibly this functional switch whereby the prose serves language first and the poem story, that gives my work its greatest definition. I didn't choose this method and the limitations of it drive me wild, but I abide, accepting in so far as I can, that I am taking the only road open to me, the only one I'm allowed to drive on this way until some unforseen detour alters my course.

In my work I'm led by my senses but I understand practical matters. I am neither interested in preserving nor exorcising the poetry of the hills. There are luminous albeit terrible facts I must simply transcribe. I the scribe. Others, transform. But on the same point, I submit you have to strike down your own mythology, about yourself, your loves, your ravishing and atavistic homeland. I am interested in the vision beyond this confrontation. Boundaries of illumination between the created, the re-created, the newly gleamed, the as yet incomprehensible. Speaking for myself, this scribbling saves me from missing a minute of what would otherwise go unspecified, unstyled. Writing is a risk and a trust. The best of it lies yonder. My linguistic skills expand on the horizon. So does the horizon. My goals are higher-minded than they once were. Once you could say, I had ambition. I never could write any old way. I would like to write so well I don't have to sever my writing from my positions; like many from my generation I desire the integrated life. Uncommitted people don't hold my interest period. Now that I have some know-how, even some readership, I'm hungrier; I don't want to break bread with the word unless convinced I have something in the mix that bears kneading. And someone to finish off the wine with, who is listening. Who is intent. Who'll read me the riot act when I shut up.

Nothing to Declare

When I lived here
the zinnias were brilliant,
spring passed in walks.
One winter I wasn't so young.
I rented a house with Ann Grey
where she wrote a book and I could not.
Cold as we were on the mountain
we wouldn't be moved to the plain.
Afternoons with no sun
a blanket is left on the line.
Hearts go bad
like something open on a shelf.
If you came to hear about roosters,
iron beds, cabinets of ruby glass —
those things are long gone;
deepscreen porches and Sunday's buffet.
This was the school
where they taught us
the Russians send their old
to be melted down for candles.
If I had a daughter I'd tell her
Go far, travel lightly.
If I had a son he'd go to war
over my hard body.
Don't tell me it isn't worth the trouble
carrying on campaigns
for the good and the dead.
The ones I would vote for
never run. I want each and every one
to rejoice in the clotheslines
of the colored peoples of the earth.
Try living where you don't have to see
the sun go down.
If the hunter turns his dogs loose
on your dreams
Start early, tell no one
get rid of the scent.

Spread Rhythm

I drift off in a panel van waiting for Isolda
to come back with coffee
so we can drive through the night.

In the roadhouse they are shoulder to shoulder.
The jukebox surrenders to the steady tread of boots,
sloshing pitchers, bright balls breaking
over the felt expanse of green.

My life an endless slum of cardboard boxes
tearing off behind us.
If we do not make the ocean
the desert can claim us
slumped over the wheel with blistered lips.

If we come to a river we'll throw our bones in.
If not we will surely drown
or, like a diamondback
curled up under the saguaro's spiky arms
doze until the cool comes.

The van yaws back onto the Interstate —
dogs barking on the overpass
of their transcendental forays
in and out of hell.

Myself, I'll wind up a crazy woman on a boat
or wake alone in the Mojave dreaming
of the Rogers boys who wore white shirts to high school
because they were going to be in finance.

I don't want so much:
a house of native rock, fruit trees
raised from seedlings, chicken in the basket
four days a week.

Wages of Love

The house is watched, the watchers only planets.

Very near the lilac
    a woman leaves her night soil
to be stepped in. Like other animals.
    Steam lifts off her mess.

    They have power, but not water.

    Pregnant. She must be.
The world is all that is the case.

You can hear the strike of the broom, a fan
    slicing overhead light.
At the table the woman stares at a dish
    of peaches, plums;
the black ants filing down the sill
    to bear away the fly.

Everywhere in America is summer. The young
    unaware they are young
their mind on other wounds
    or the new music.

The heart some bruised fruit
knocked loose by a long stick
    aches at the stem.
It's not forbidden to fall out of love
    like from a tree.

As for the tenants whose waters will break
    in this bed
May they live through the great pain;
may their offspring change everything —

    Because everything must change.

The man joins the woman in the kitchen.
They touch the soft place of their fruit.
They enter in, tell their side and pass through.

The world is all that is the case.

Provinces

Where the old trees reign with their forward dark
light stares through a hole in the body's long
house. The bed rolls away from the body,
and the body is forced to find a chair. At some hour
the body sequesters itself in a shuttered room
with no clock. When a clean sheet of paper floats by,
the head inclines on its axis. It is one of those
common bodies that felt it could not exist without loving,
but has in fact gone on and on without love.
Like a cave that has stopped growing, we don't call it dead,
but dormant. Now the body is on all fours, one arm
engaged in pulling hair from a trap, an activity
the body loathes. When the time comes, the body
feeds on marinated meats and fruits trained to be luscious.
Once the body had ambitions — to be tall and remain
soft. No more, but it enjoys rappelling to the water.
Because the body's dwelling is stone, perched over water,
we say the body is privileged. Akin to characters
in Lawrence books, its livelihood is obscured. It owns
a horse named Campaign it mounts on foggy morns.
That was the body's first lie. It has no horse
and wouldn't climb on one. Because the body lives
so far from others, it likes reading about checkered lives
in the metropoli. It likes moving around at night under its dress.
When it travels, bottles of lotion open in its bags.
Early in March the big rains came — washing all good thoughts
from the body's cracks and chinks. By now the body admits
it is getting on, and yet, continues to be tormented
by things being the way they are. Recently the body took
one of the old trees for a wife, but the union has broken down.
The light has bored out of the body's long house.
Fog envelops its stone flanks. Still the body
enjoys rapelling to the water. And it likes the twenty-four stores,
walking up and down the aisles, not putting a thing in its basket.

Glowworm

We go singly and by threes,
we pair off I to I.
You winter, he springs, she summers;
the dish runs away with the spoon.
She throws a knife at the wall.
In a year, the spoon comes back
without the dish,
the knife cools off in a drawer.

Further on down the road
(a record hot afternoon)
a man is having some pie
in a diner with a platinum top.
His boy sleeps in their car

breathing through the mouth.
The man talks about leaving this country
because the country's gone to dogs.
He raps his quarter on the counter.
Somebody plays J6, BamalamaBamaloo.
Behind the gleaming hull of the diner

a transparent river rustles by;
the weeping cherries and weeping willows
and grass known as widow's hair
begin to sway. Pretty soon,
the moon takes a shift for the sun.
The father avoids the clock.

The boy with the head cold
can't hear the stars burning on and off.
The moon nudges under his snap-button shirt
to swab his front with its menthol,
barely misting his tender genitalia
with its chronic desire.

Little Sisters

This was to be called *Rojo*; there were to be hot combs, hanks of hair in flames, seven whores of Memphis taking their oath in night court. But they have left the image area without so much as a whambamthankyoumaa'm;

I am thrown back on a house built right in the twister's path (shortly before it struck): When Snake Maynard was starting out, things must have been different. He would look in his medicine chest just to admire the shapely bottles and jars. If he stepped out of doors, brooder houses to the front, brooder houses to the rear; feathers blowing down the government's right-of-way. There were many givens: he knew the pensioner would be getting up before light, lathering up his dark jaw. He would slap his face with astringent, tuck the aluminum thermos under the wool shirt. And step out. He knew the woman who wouldn't sell her gallon container of assorted buttons was touched. Everyone said so, She's touched. And he knew Mr. Wallace of Lock & Key was dying of lung cancer; that he had his Pall Malls delivered. Before the doctor made his call Mr. Wallace wore a shower cap (so the hair wouldn't smell). In this green town under gaping stars no one went anonymously hungry. Almost nobody murdered another. Ribbons of smoke unraveling from the chimney. The shingles sparkle under the sun. Women go to basements with a load of white then a load of colored clothes. Secretly they drink. Yes, yes. Written in fire on my forehead, the fine-pointed ways of the first boy I screwed. His far and gone look (the wisdom of those who die young). He used to lie awake with his arms behind his head. Like so. I would be having the dream of falling ladders. Thousands of butterflies crossed the Atlantic. All of my enemies in robes.

Perhaps a better title is *How Life Should Be Lived* by Spanish Olive. I took my name from a pizza ingredient. I am the acquitted. Lost pleiade. Snake Maynard was a personal friend. And if I make it back with the shoplifted ham I know our imaginary daughter could be doing The Locomotive to the noise the refrigerator makes. She too lives an essential life, and one of genius in the field of love. The other day she phoned to say hello, meaning she had a dream about me.

Vestigial Love Poem

A woman stands on the roof of her car
pounding a stake into the earth
with a rock.
If she had post hole diggers
her job on this land would be done.
She half hopes her husband doesn't come,
the professor, in his suit . . .
the stain dilating under her arms.
But before dark he drives up
to see her light into smiles —
his back thoughts imploding
like a television —
to bring some news.
So there they were
with the black cords that hang from the heart
hanging fire, fused.
And this is where they dropped down in the dirt
and dug with their lives
with rock for a bed
a nice hole
in which to lay
their perfectly lonely egg.

for Michael and for Shirley

Ancestor Figure

The road split off like odd ends of rope.
All roads led to Grove where a Sinclair
would stand. Not a week before the incident,
the river crested, houses tumbled down banks.
Cats were wailing in top limbs.
But on the day in question, Robert took the tracks.
He didn't want a wagon hurling gumbo on his suit —
worn to Dee's shivaree, Lester's wake; worn
day of the incident and this one, to Court.
He took a gentleman's pride in dress
meaning he did not work. Nor did Robert
drink. Cavort. Smoke. Thief. Cheat at stud.
He carried protection. Like any man.
The morn in question was a numinous one. Fields
drifting in bluets. And he loved to walk.
He recalled tonguing the hole in his jaw.
And whistling to make himself stop.
The pure reservoir of sky let only the bluest
light pass through its increasing depths . . .
and them little niggers. Them dam kids —
as whites called the dam builders' offspring.
Robert was heading toward Grove
on his side of the rails. They were headed
for the dam camp. They bore sacks.
And they veered. They, the dam kids,
veered, and he, Robert, fired.
                                   Of course
this occurred long before any of us lived
to pause over poor Robert's skull,
the dam kids, twins, not yet nine;
the numinous forenoon, fields drifting in bluets
through which Adrian and Dorian bore sacks.

The Complete Birth Of The Cool

Under this sun voices on the radio run down,
ponds warp like a record.
In the millyard men soak; roses hang from the neck.
Everyone is thankful for dusk
and the theater's blue tubes of light.
But evenings are a non-church matter.
On the cement step — damp from my swimming suit
I sort out my life or not,
an illustrated dictionary on my lap.
If I want hamburger I make it myself
Behind the wrapped pipes
Sister expels a new litter
in the crawlspace. Even she can see
the moon poling across the water
to guard the giant melon in my patch.
Awe provides for us.

Treatment

This a 16mm film of 7 minutes in which no words are spoken. But for a few hand-tinted elements: the girl's dress, the sax, sky at church, the color is black and white. The camera reports in the all-knowing third except in handheld shots when it momentarily exposes the driver's field of vision.

The bus rocks out of ruts and over creek rocks at pre-dawn. The driver hasn't picked up any children. He has the radio on and a cigarette lit. Isn't paying attention to either. His headlights scan the road, and webs in the trees, as if they were searchlights. His mind is bent as his posture and his face reveal. A girl dresses in purple in the dark. She feels along the wallpaper to the kitchen, fixes oatmeal, warms coffee to which she adds globs of honey. She makes a sandwich for lunch. She starts to eat out of the pot on the stove. Stops and gets a bowl from a high cabinet and sits at the table. She taps with her foot to a tune she hums only inside herself. When she goes back upstairs to comb her hair and make an irregular part; to tinkle, she hears her parents. Their bedsprings. A shot of them under many covers. Apparently her mother has told her she is a love child. She understands so her listening isn't upsetting. She steals in her younger brother's room and leaves a bird she has folded from one sheet of paper on the nightstand. When she hears the bus shifting at the foot of the hill she grabs sweater and tablet and flies past the lunchsack on the banister. Their house isn't beautiful but its shadows are. The driver greets her with Hey Princess. That look. She sits close to the rear. The driver climbs the hill and puts it in neutral under an elm stand. He jerks the handbrake. The camera is in back and shooting forward as he comes down the aisle — it is behind her. He looms larger than he is and walks as if the bus were in motion. The rape is explicit. The camera shoots out the back and side windows every few seconds to see if anyone, another vehicle, approaches. There are no more shots of the girl. The parents' house is shown from the yard and from the foot of her window. Light breaks in the trees, a cool sun. You hear the bus grind, the children, as the bus fills and proceeds. Then a field of high grass, a white church. No roads leading there. No cars parked nearby. Slight quality of a different world. A saxophone is played. A full choir accompanies. A silent congregation, all stand, motionless. All adults.

Pharoah Sanders stands in front of the choir stall in white robes. He plays with his eyes shut. He plays a curved soprano. His foot taps to an interior beat. Clearly he's an Angel. With the horn he lures. Accuses. His solo has a timeless aura. The doors of the church blow open. The driver falls onto the aisle. He begins to squirm on his belly toward the Pharoah. It is a long journey. The Pharoah wails controllably. The choir sways, claps; the congregation keeps quiet, light breaks in the trees and indistinct voices of many children fill the nave as if they were boarding a bus.

The Spirit Hunter

A child wakes in a wide bed, tasting the nest
in her gums. There are traces of wet feather,
tiny bones. She watches the wallpaper.
Nothing flies off. Then she walks in her pajamas
to the sidewalk's end, calling her cat. Mr. Reynolds
stands in the four o'clocks. Immaculate.
Never late or on time. She rubs her eyes.
*Tie my steed to this tree and shake me
down some figs before I steal on out of here,*
his very words. When the parent wanted to know
who could she be talking to so early
she told, *Oh he had some dew, then he left.*
She thought better of mentioning his lachrymose horse.

Acoustics

There was so much more to be said.
But to whom would she say so.

The woman ate all the light meat
then she pushed her plate and water glass away
and made up her mind to take the freight lift.

The Seven Sisters would be visible
she read in the evening news
for everyone living outside the *lueur.*

The spirit-filled gentleman offered her
cash for the dog; he offered
to bring 100 of his 1500 angels with him
when he came for the dog
as though he were herding them, angels.

A clean brush and comb,
folding clothes hot from the dryer,
a letter to the editor in her best hand
— These things she took pleasure in,
beautiful deeds: anonymous, completed.

That music again, pushing the cold strings
as if with blistered fingers.

The old woman in her remembers the lithe: summers
on Lake Return. The wide lip of bluff, catching
bugs, barbeque. Judge snagging his tie
in the ice cream churn; the dresses her mother wore.
And in long grass, the dead lion she thought she saw.

Then she is having the dream
of falling figures, but is not harmed
counting herself among those who fly.

Carla

The old man in my mind
squats under a shedding locust
drinking water still cold from a gourd.
Never has he seen an orange
growing on a tree.
You could not pay him
to go where they grow.
His desire as it has been
since he can remember
is to keep pure for her.
As if he were young and light, not changed.
So that she will want him
again as in the very beginning.
He sees so much to paint
if he painted.
Yes he could back the Desoto
out of the shed, coast to the blacktop.
And drive until he ran out of cash
or splendor.

Slag

The orange rivers and red dogs of Paul Gauguin
do not run through these hills.
The light that caught us here, the crazy quilts
were drawn in charcoal.
Days colder than night
avoid the foggy eyes of the clock.
This is the chilling winter of our lives.
Forty wives make forty widows.
Deep in a wound of earth
someone coughs. All of him strains
to breathe; to hear
the insomniac echo of her naked feet
as she walks the hard floor to the pump.
At the sink, she gulps from her hand.
Behind her devoted black oak
the mineralized sky weakening, glows.

Elements of Night

Cold food, homework and hair. Rooms with a radiator and no books. Moths like flour. Venetian blinds. Wallets tossed from cars. Cockeye. Fish do not slow down. A good robe. Pencils. The back of his head. Breeze. Scene in another language. Beds hard as boards. A girl climbing a fence like a vine. Records left out of covers. Moving furniture. Cleaning women. Clocks. A praying mantis in a jar. Barns blown down. Her rainy underarms. Faith hope and hypocrisy. Trees growing old. Boats in fields. Guests. A box on fire. Icetrays. Ironing. Genitals like underwater fruit. People drinking out of a bottle. Urine. Crimes of passion. Mascara. Valet parking. A small college green. Adjustable lamp. *Even the way she holds her neck.* Trailers. Slamming doors. Fine rugs, baby grand. Change for the phone. a polalic version. Jobs taken on the lam. Radar. A bad mole. Unpublished number. Houses you can't see from the road. Television. The glory hole. Now that visiting hours are over. Musicians on break. A novel like a neighbor. Vestibules of mirrors and light. Sprayed on a wall: Leo dies alone. Also: 1981, Where is my beautiful daughter.

Hotels

In the semi-dark we take everything off,
love standing, inaudible; then we crawl into bed.
You sleep with your head balled up in its dreams,
I get up and sit in the chair with a warm beer
the lamp off. Looking down on a forested town
in a snowfall I feel like a novel — dense
and vivid, uncertain of the end — watching
the bundled outlines of another woman another man
hurrying toward the theater's blue tubes of light.

The Wooden Age

It is afternoon. One hour earlier there, whole as a hen. The oaks browned weeks before the rest, ready for sweeping into the covers dragged from a married brother's bed.... Here am I lifted out of my natural hellbroth and wrapped in the used foil of belching stacks, chop shops and storage tanks; served up on the gaslit hill to a private school, where it is privately fall just above the private library and club for men, flecked into the tweeds of their private humidor, pushing carved pieces of wood around a chequered board;

cutting through the park, I watch families of Hmong foraging greens, mushrooms and some long stalk from recreational waters. A woman and her girl, fish from the lake stocked with tires and yellow kittens;

were I wheeling out of Birdtown's pine and bloodroot, I would stop at the one-pump station beyond kilns where they fire charcoal briquets, and the training center for wayward boys,

or accelerate toward a concrete bridge spanning the Buffalo and the iron bridge that runs beside it; the prosperous motel on the far banks of the river, the ruined one on the near where snakes impersonate the copperheaded bluff — to where the vestigial wild cat, having sprung out of a sassafrass to fight from its back, lost to the vestigial wildman, was bagged and brought down

town — if you want to call it one. Every store on Main dark and sold to a manufacturer of uniforms. The blue uniformed workers sewing their own blues like prisoners who build their own cells. Even Old Man Reuther had to die and his widow to wither and be bought out, and that was the last horehound stick; that was when the cowbells came down from the two-story doors of Reuther's House of Three Wonders: you wonder if we have it, we wonder if we don't, we both wonder if we can find it.

Living in the autumn afternoon: a woman might set up a table in the shade, the pastor call on someone tied to their bed, impatiens blooming yet in black iron washpots; a man tell his spouse for anyone in earshot that when her mother went to the hospital, the fleas lost their host. O my rotting trout dock, Old Capital Theater, taxidermy and beauty school, Sunday immersions. O Gazo's Bait Shop, Cady St. Cafe, biscuits and gravy, furniture barns, lightning-split elm, o book mobile, notions, rocks, light bread, cigarettes and pop . . . .

Eleven miles west, in the commercial center, they are dreaming about having their face lifted, their soft butt tucked; the men are losing their hair and cleaning out their desk to make themselves feel better. They don't hear paint peel and the garden overgrowing. In one of those lives I was a mimosa shooting up unplanted by the tracks. Either that or a yard chicken, more of a pet than something for the pot. Or was I learning lip reading at home, in case I needed it

in the city: just when you start in on that souther bird, the buzzard, in a land of uncertain springs, the shift whistle sounds. This is where we get up and go piss on the bricks; drive off throwing chain-food wrappers out the window . . .

This is where we lug our burning brains to feed the tree.

Lapse

After the last war we drafted pages and pages
of our final will and testimony. Then we set off
in a different direction. What we left behind
didn't amount to much. I was all for living
the fictitious life. We chipped in to drive
until we ran out of gas. We wound up in one lost valley.
Cold cash passed through us like lightning through trees.
We nearly died laughing. We weren't drunk.
Winter was mild, the spring came in torrents.
Under the duck cloth with handkerchiefs on our heads —
due to a hat shortage — there was talk of building
a spur back to the main highway. Our jokes
wore thin, our jeans. We printed a paper
by night, the single issue being peace.
Water oaks in the carlights looked like I don't know what.
We slept fine; the cooking wasn't bad.
The part I remember fondly: him,
sitting up in the semi-naked sunshine,
his hair blowing all around.

Scratch Music

How many threads have I broken with my teeth. How many times
have I looked at the stars and felt ill. Time here is divided into before
and since your shuttering in 1978. I remember hanging onto the
hood of the big-fendered Olds with a mess of money in my purse.
Call that romance. Some memory precedes you: when I wanted
lederhosen because I'd read *Heidi*. And how I wanted my folks to
build a fall-out shelter so I could arrange the cans. And coveting
mother's muskrat. I remember college. And being in Vista: I asked
the librarian in Banks, the state's tomato capitol, if she had any black
literature and she said they used to have *Lil Black Sambo* but the white
children tore out pages and wrote ugly words inside. Someone said
if I didn't like Banks I should go to Moscow. I said, Come on, let's go
outside and shoot the hoop. I've got a jones to beat your butt. I haven't
changed. Now if I think of the earth's origins, I get vertigo. When I
think of its death, I fall. I've picked up a few things. I know if you
want songbirds, plant berry trees. If you don't want birds, buy a
rubber snake. I remember that town with the Alcoa plant I toured.
The manager kept referring to the workers as Alcoans. I thought of
hundreds of flexible metal beings bent over assemblages. They
sparked. What would I do in Moscow. I have these dreams — relatives
loom over my bed. We should put her to sleep Lonnie says. Go home
old girl, go home, my aunt says. Why should I go home before her I
want to say. But I am bereft. So how is Life in The Other World. Do
you get the news. Are you allowed a pet. But I wanted to show you
how I've grown, what I know: I keep my bees far from the stable,
they can't stand how horses smell. And I know sooner or later an old

house will need a new roof. And more than six years have whistled by since you blew your heart out like the porchlight. Reason and meaning don't step into another lit spot like a well-meaning stranger with a hat. And mother's mother who has lived in the same house ten times six years, told me, We didn't know we had termites until they swarmed. Then we had to pull up the whole floor. 'Too late, no more...,' you know the poem. But you, you bastard. You picked up a gun in winter as if it were a hat and you were leaving a restaurant: full, weary, and thankful to be spending the evening with no one.

Illuminations

I have heard of one man of atonement:
in a tent on a frozen lake
under the aurora australis, he sleeps
in his down, dreaming of no one,
his airplane. There is the oil
he guards with his body. The lamp
at his back like another body,
someone with a sun inside of her.
A gloved finger rubs a blue eyelid.
There is horror first of the life
that goes on below ice. By degrees
the limbs harden with light. Thinking
of a word no longer spoken by men:
Vouchsafe.

The Legend of Hell

A few hours ago a woman went on a walk.
Her phone rang and rang.
What a pleasure, she said to herself,
To walk in the fields and pick walnuts.

A moment ago a white dog
whose chain snared a shopping cart,
barked and barked.
Someone sauntered through an orchard
with murdering the whole family on his mind.

At the Black Pearl dancing was nightly.
That Sonnyman showed up again,
too tall for his clothes.
The pretentious copper beech threw its final shadow
on the D.A.'s house. Where we were living,
you wouldn't dream of going unaccompanied.

A few hours ago you could be at the movies,
borrow a comb from a stranger.
In the cities you had your braille libraries;
couples dining on crustacean
with precious instruments. In the provinces
you had your jug bands, anabaptists sharing their yield.

Then comes the wolf:
in a room of a house on a plain
lie the remains of Great Aunt Gladys

the quintessential Bell operator
sent many a rose by many a party in pain.

(By remains, we mean depression
left by her big body on her high bed);
over here we have an early evening scene without figures,
the soft parts of children blown into trees.
Our neighbors are putting on their prettiest things.
Their clocks have stopped but all hearts calibrated.

They say they are ready now
to make their ascension into light.
And you Edward Teller we know you're out there
shelling nuts; saying to yourself alone,
Now this is a pleasure.

homage to Barbara McClintock

Kahlo

She must have made her way from the mezzanine with a monkey on her shoulder; limped through those arches looking for a cigarette her fan of skirts sweeping the washed tile. She loved to smoke and talk nasty. She was in permanent pain. In costume from bed to sea. I missed her in Mexico. Long before I sucked a breath out of this courtyard she was one dead soldadera.

Imagine: the fruit was green and cold, the moon hot as wax. Someone else poured. She barely drank. She was nearly beautiful. They must have been at one of these tables. When you set your glass down your face appears obliquely. They were six, seven including the Frenchman in a black shirt. Not the saboteur, a comrade. The mariachis hung back in the foliage like gourds. Trotsky talked: how everyone would paint and there would be no painters, fondling her crumpled leg under the cloth. She was twenty-nine. He wouldn't see sixty again. Rivera came down heavily from the scaffold. He opened his arms like a wide net. Here, she ate with her fingers — the famous fishes of Patzcuaro flipping down her tilted neck and in their wake, a hatch of dragonflies.

We've come from a city of tortilla lines to a town of ribby dogs and dolorous bells. The healer and I put my husband to bed. We give him something to help him remember boyhood poems and forget work, something to blacken the hair, cure envy and bad airs. Whether man's heart is mutable, woman's will mend. If he were Frida we would offer him many American cigarettes, quartered melon, a special brush for her ramous eyebrow.

The Lesson

This is the chair. This is the lamp. Here is your pencil. The switch is over there. That book lives in the drawer. You speak well. The mirror doesn't work. Those bracelets belonged to a former guest. She had two children she saw only once in a while. Then she wore shadow and silver. Your bed is good and hard. The fruit is cool and dark. People are friendly here. The barman has information to burn. If the moon becomes too much you can close this gown. From the gallery you see the big lights of our Holy Father's summer place, and the flower farms. The lake turns purple from the fertilizer. It is so lovely, it is a pity the fish have to go belly up. The other woman kept a boa for a pet. When her children came she would glisten and alternately glow. Leave your soiled things where you will. Service is complete. You enjoy typing. I can tell. If you wake up bleeding from the mouth, use the spider's web as a styptic. Would your hair be red everywhere. She was what you call a bottle blond. Not a true blond. In the beginning, she was fervent, more fervent, most fervent. Try staying in the vocative case. That window has been painted shut. The radio is for your listening and dancing pleasure. Do you cotton to Dixieland. Excuse my little joke. You will have to share a toilet with a man who plucks his eyebrows. Allow me. Please, that is very heavy. Let me. Would you like to make a long distance telephone call. Do you rent a safety deposit box also. You see we are very modernaire. Did you observe as you came in, the Monument to Tomorrow. Is this the first time you are having your face peeled.

The Rio

Because we know who we are
what we want from life
and who we should kill to get it,
we are up with the first shot of light
combing hanks, wiping front to rear;

                       in Mexico
the rosary of beans and tortillas
comes before the catechism
of pulque and bruises,

whereas we razor, don hosiery; then
whoosh to warm up our amative cars
before putting them on the pike.
                       In Mexico
the day falls in soft plops,
everybody labors
under the sun's fork and its yolk.

But there is no need to diddle the knobs —
between carpet land and tire world
and the new plant where body bags are seamed —
or touch a blessed thing. Us.
Only cruise, sidle into an authorized spot.
                       In Mexico
a man paddles into a cantina
under a urinous moon proclaiming
this rooster cost the eye out of my face,
but up here we feel this points to
a coarseness to discuss prices.

This Couple

Now is when we love to sit before mirrors
with a dark beer or hand out leaflets
at chainlink gates or come together after work
listening to each other's hard day. The engine dies,
no one hurries to go in. We might
walk around in the yard not making a plan.
The freeway is heard but there's no stopping
progress, and the week has barely begun. Then
we are dressed. It rains. Our heads rest
against the elevator wall inhaling a stranger;
we think of cliffs we went off
with our laughing friends. The faces
we put our lips to. Our wonderful sex
under whatever we wear. And of the car
burning on the side of the highway. Of jukeboxes
we fed. Quarters circulating with our prints.
Things we sent away for. Long drives. The rain. Cafes
where we ate late and once only. Eyes of an animal
in the headlamps. The guestbooks that verify
our whereabouts. Your apple core in the ashtray.
The pay toilets where we sat without paper. Rain.
Articles left with former lovers. The famous
ravine of childhood. Movie lines we've stood in
when it really came down. Moments
we have felt forsaken: waiting for the others
to step from the wrought iron compartment,
or passing through some town with the dial
on a Mexican station, wondering for the life of us,
where are we going and when would we meet.

The Cinematographer's Färo Island Log

Like so many stories this begins
with a house harbored under larch;
a bag of green tea dropped over the rim
of a handed-down cup.

It begins with the pale husband, limited light;
fingers parting the labium
and her ear in his mouth.

Soon, the man is downstairs with a towel,
the peripatetic camera at his heels.

They will dress in darkness for work,
him going without shoes in the house
like the Japanese girl he loved first.

He stares at the lake carved like a mirror
and listens to the sough of her comb —
one hundred strokes of night.

The camera studies the venation of new leaves
on a lightning-split tree near shore.

The tea is greener now and cold.
The woman he married is seated
before the mirror. She stares
through concentric circles in the glass

and asks of the figure leaving
the shadowy cove of their hall,
What is your favorite body of water. And why.

Petition For Replenishment

We do not mean to complain. We know how it is.
In older, even sadder cultures the worst possible sorts
have been playing hot and cold with people's lives
for much longer. Like Perrow says,
We'll all have baboon hearts one of these days.
We wintered with ample fuel and real tomatoes.
We were allowed to roam, sniffing and chewing
at the tufted crust. We were let to breathe.
That is, we respirated. Now the soft clocks
have gorged themselves on our time. Yet
as our hair blanches and comes out
in hanks, we can tell it is nearly spring —
the students shed their black coats
on the green; we begin to see shade.
Lo, this is the breastbone's embraceable light.
We are here. Still beating and constellated.

One Summer

Not even Goldie could have told
— with her talent for telling —
I would sit here at the end
of the wild broom in my wrinkled linen,
Lives of the Artists on my knees,
a window open on flowering tobacco fields
and the ancient Antolini farmhouse;
she could not have pictured me
so peaceable and sound,
defecating merrily under the wheeze
of Arnoldo's accordian
against the whick of Mita's deft sickle.

Two Hearts In A Forest

Evening Shade

I am over here, by the tomato cages
gently touching the wire,
watching one lightning bug light another
freshly fucked and childless
an astonished woman in a wedding gown
who can see in the dark, almost.

Lush Life

I could have gone to Stringtown
O I could have wasted away
moaning in the swamped bed
among winged roaches and twisted figs
between the fern and dark thighs.

Hotel Philharmonic

We have arrived drunk, jobless,
brilliant with love.
Music commences:
You hold out your glass
I lift my dress. My hands
saved like candles for a storm
in yours. We fall
through the night's caesura.

Lost Roads

As though following a series of clues, we drove
through this ragged range, a town of magnetic springs
our arms in the window, browning.
The sun was torching the hair of maples
You didn't sing in key, you sang
Famous Blue Raincoat.
I had a dream, Life isn't real.
Already the sad rapture entering.

Mountain Herald

This time, the Celebrant vowed, No one would intinct,
blowing the unsteady flames of our face.
We rose and married well, my nose
in your tender swarthiness. I'll never forget
the whirling floor, the bassman's royal head.
As for the uninvited they were asked in.
Melon, not cake was served;
there was japonica and spirea. Still
they were a little late for the forsythia,
God yes, the forsythia, forsythia.

2 April, 1983

Handfasting

It says in Wednesday's *Journal:* a woman, 85, went out
for the mail. Fell. The man, 92, went out to help. Fell.
Both froze on their walk. Your body strewn over the quilt
makes me think of meat pulled from a shell.
When I am every bit of 92, you will be only 85.
I don't mean to be unfeeling toward their surviving boy.
But it struck me, a stranger, as one of love's merciful ends.
Desirous even. I want us to live for that assignation.
I want us to rise with the first crib of light
like a milky new mother and husband; step out
as if for mail, and freeze our flabby asses off together.

Further Adventures With You

We are on a primeval river in a reptilian den.

There are birds you don't want to tangle with, trees
    you cannot identify...

Somehow we spend the evening with Mingus
in a White Castle. Or somewhere. Nearly drunk. He says
he would like to play for the gang.

All of us ride to Grandmother Wright's house
in a van. It's her old neighborhood. I think we look
like a carton of colas sitting up stiffly
    behind the glass.

She is recently dead. Some of her belongings
are gone. Her feather mattress has been rolled back
from the springs. It turns out Mingus has forgotten
his cello. We lay on our sides in jackets and jeans
    as if it were a beach in fall.

Then it is Other Mama's house. She is
recently dead. We stretch out on Other Mama's carpet
    pulling at its nap.

You and I have stomped into A-Mart to buy papers
and Schnapps. Two boys, one pimply, the other clear-skinned
    blow in like snow with blue handkerchiefs
and a gun. Blue is the one color I notice tonight.
    They tell us, Take off.

We're gone. We're on the back of the bus with the liquor.
    The silly boys have shot the package store clerk.
We're the only suspects. You have a record so you're in a sweat.
You're flashing black, white. Around the nose and mouth

you remind me a little of Sam Cooke. I think
he was shot in a motel. A case of sexual madness. We get off
at an old bar that shares a wall with a school for girls.

The police collar us there. They separate us for questioning.
You show a work card that swears you're a male dancer.
You pull out a gun. Where did you get that. And you blast them.
It's their hearts, I think My god.

You yell out a non-word and hit the doors. I run
through the back. It's the girls school. They seem to be
getting ready
for a revue. I try to blend in — hoist a mattress, somebody's music
up a staircase. There are racks of costumes on wheels,
flats of moving scenery . . .

There is the river, the horrible featherless bird. The tree,
not a true palm but of the palm family.

On The Eve Of Our Mutually Assured Destruction

we were not even moving. No one was moving.
We had the windows rolled
so we could hear. No one was hurt. They
were working on the bridge. A woman
held the sign: men working. The radio was beat.
Somebody must have ripped off the aerial
in the lot. Wednesday, March 6: wind shovelling fog.
We were talking about going to another place...
until the worst was over...where insects nest
in the ears of convolvuli, clear soups are imbibed.
We didn't have change. Not a bill.
After the bridge came the tunnel, then
the toll. We felt so lonesome we wanted to cry.
The couple ahead of us lit up.
Their baby thrashed in its carrier.
We talked about following
the migration of protected beings.
We wanted to leap or turn around. There
could be no turning around. We would get rid
of the chairs and the stoneware. Find a home
for the black mollies. We would rent
bicycles in an old town under a machicolated wall.
Clatter over cobbles in public health specs
arguing about Trotsky. Like thirties' poets.
Yes there would be the dense canopy,
the floor of mosses, liverworts and ferns.
I would open my legs like a book
letting the soft pencils of light
fall on our pages, like doors
into a hothouse, cereus blooming there.
I would open up like a wine list, a mussel, wings

to be mounted without tearing.
I would part my legs in the forest
and let the fronds impress themselves in the resin
of my limbs; smoothe your rump
like a horse's. To wit the whole world would not be lost.

Apparent Dimensions Of Celestial Bodies

Another day here, still but not long.
The light came early as a girl, so I'm up, drinking
from the tap. I go into my footlocker with a stick.
Mine is the room next to the crapper. Always overflowing.
Talk about angels, they seem suspicious to me,
their radiant lapels, shit-eating smiles. In the warm wax
of my back they dug this inscription: Say it
with flowers. O sometimes I might look on my life
on the planet, long but never still.
I wasn't sent to foretell the Return of the Son, Withering
of the State. No, they armed me strictly with facts:
My 5th grade boyfriend is an undertaker, the Price farm
a firing range; all things lovely and equal
are more likely to be eaten and lethal
than in our written history.

So, take it breeze, green leaves:

Only once I went back among the trees I blew down from.
I was in a fix to see Home. My head drifted
into the pillows on Spring Street and I listened.
I can't tell you... the milk bottles clinked together
banded with cream; there were the large red roses
in the kitchen giving up a petal selfless as the old
making love, and Great Uncle Walker
who saw communists in his soup, slipping me a buck
for a song. It was he who fought
his lifelong friend to their deaths in the field

with a sickle and a saw over the ownership of a hog.
The families sorted their remains
like old socks, nearest match.
The species has a ways yet, wouldn't you say so.

Look up, there's no money on the floor. What we need
is a little snake oil, a tour through the City of Lights,
one more trot to the Original Inkspots. Never mind
the sharpshooters along the boulevard
invisible and full of glory.
See here how the morning commences
with the beautiful circumstance of freshly cut blades.

Carnegie-Mellon Poetry

1975

The Living and the Dead, Ann Hayes
In the Face of Descent, T. Alan Broughton

1976

The Week the Dirigible Came, Jay Meek
Full of Lust and Good Usage, Stephen Dunn

1977

*How I Escaped from the Labyrinth and
    Other Poems,* Philip Dacey
The Lady from the Dark Green Hills, Jim Hall
For Luck: Poems 1962-1977, H.L. Van Brunt
By the Wreckmaster's Cottage, Paula Rankin

1978

New & Selected Poems, James Bertolino
The Sun Fetcher, Michael Dennis Browne
A Circus of Needs, Stephen Dunn
The Crowd Inside, Elizabeth Libbey

1979

Paying Back the Sea, Philip Dow
Swimmer in the Rain, Robert Wallace
Far From Home, T. Alan Broughton
The Room Where Summer Ends, Peter Cooley
No Ordinary World, Mekeel McBride

1980

*And the Man Who Was Traveling Never Got
    Home,* H.L. Van Brunt

Drawing on the Walls, Jay Meek
The Yellow House on the Corner, Rita Dove
The 8-Step Grapevine, Dara Wier
The Mating Reflex, Jim Hall

1981
A Little Faith, John Skoyles
Augers, Paula Rankin
Walking Home from the Icehouse, Vern Rutsala
Work and Love, Stephen Dunn
The Rote Walker, Mark Jarman
Morocco Journal, Richard Harteis
Songs of a Returning Soul, Elizabeth Libbey

1982
The Granary, Kim R. Stafford
Calling the Dead, C.G. Hanzlicek
Dreams Before Sleep, T. Alan Broughton
Sorting It Out, Anne S. Perlman
*Love Is Not a Consolation; It Is a
   Light,* Primus St. John

1983
*The Going Under of the
   Evening Land,* Mekeel McBride
Museum, Rita Dove
Air and Salt, Eve Shelnutt
Nightseasons, Peter Cooley

1984

Falling From Stardom, Jonathan Holden
Miracle Mile, Ed Ochester
Girlfriends and Wives, Robert Wallace
Earthly Purposes, Jay Meek
Not Dancing, Stephen Dunn
The Man in the Middle, Gregory Djanikian
A Heart Out of This World, David James
All You Have in Common, Dara Wier

1985

Smoke From the Fires, Michael Dennis Browne
Full of Lust and
    Good Usage, Stephen Dunn (2nd edition)
Far and Away, Mark Jarman
Anniversary of the Air, Michael Waters
To the House Ghost, Paula Rankin
Midwinter Transport, Anne Bromley

1986

Seals in the Inner Harbor, Brendan Galvin
Thomas and Beulah, Rita Dove
Further Adventures With You, C.D. Wright